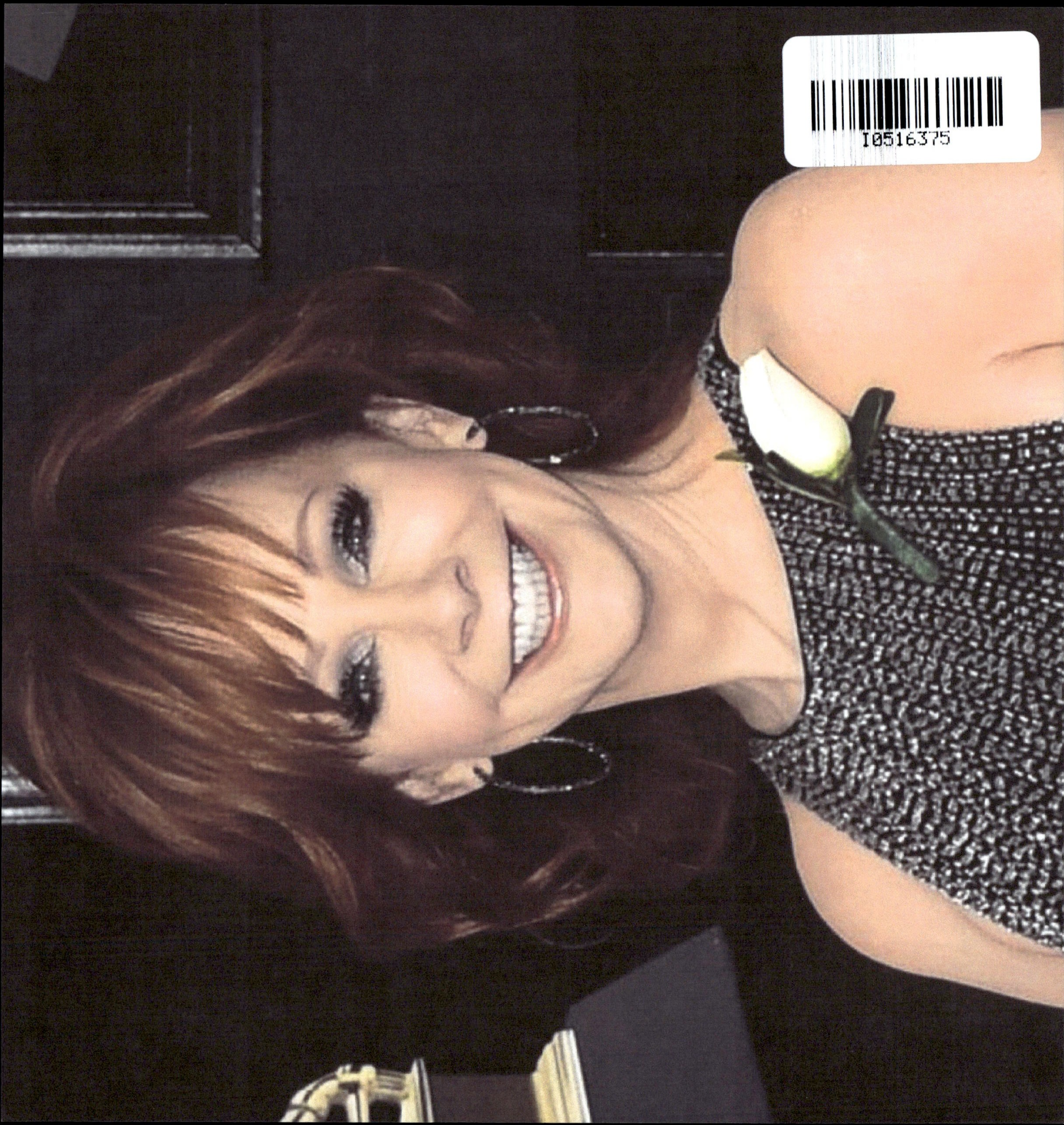

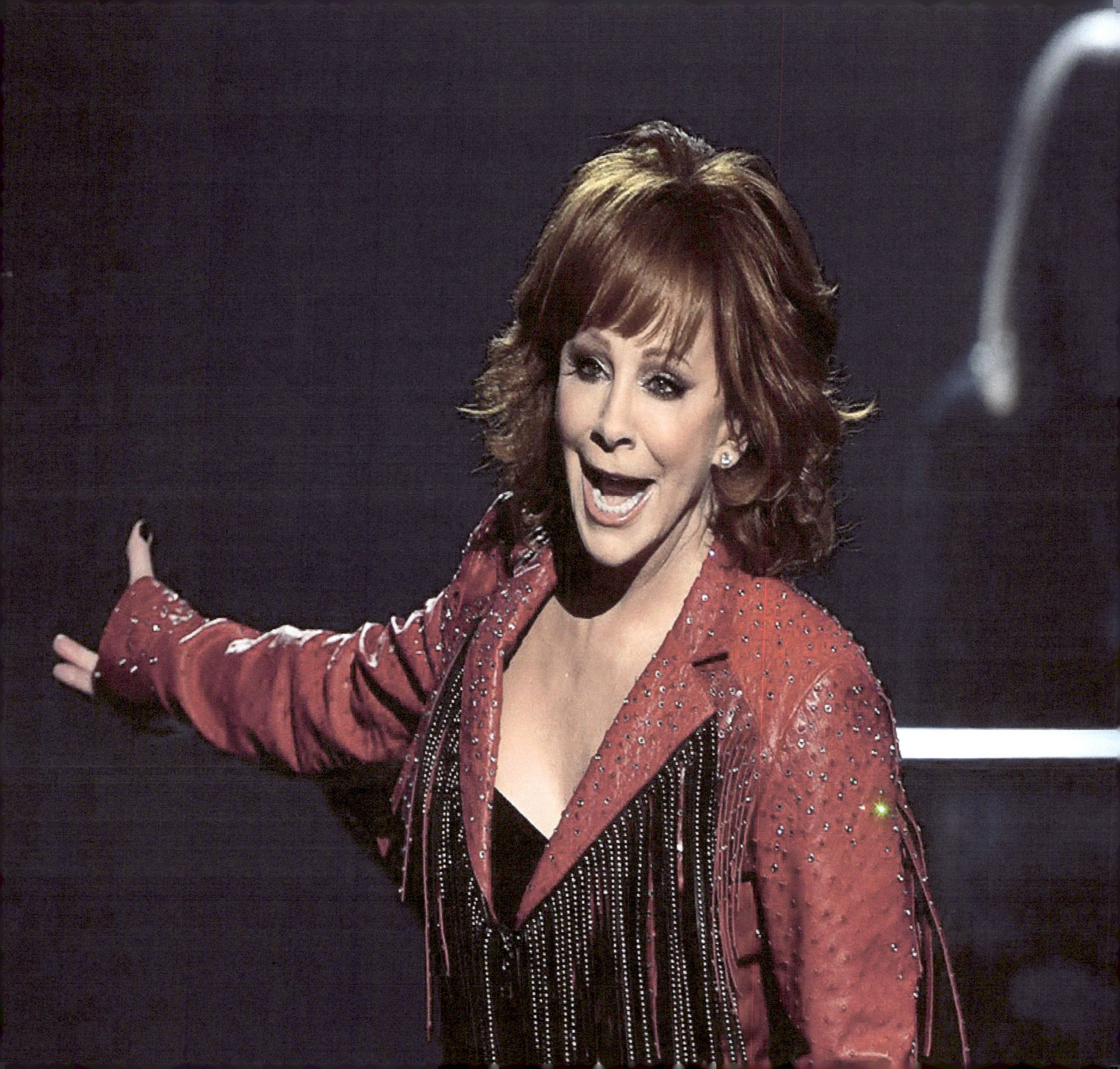

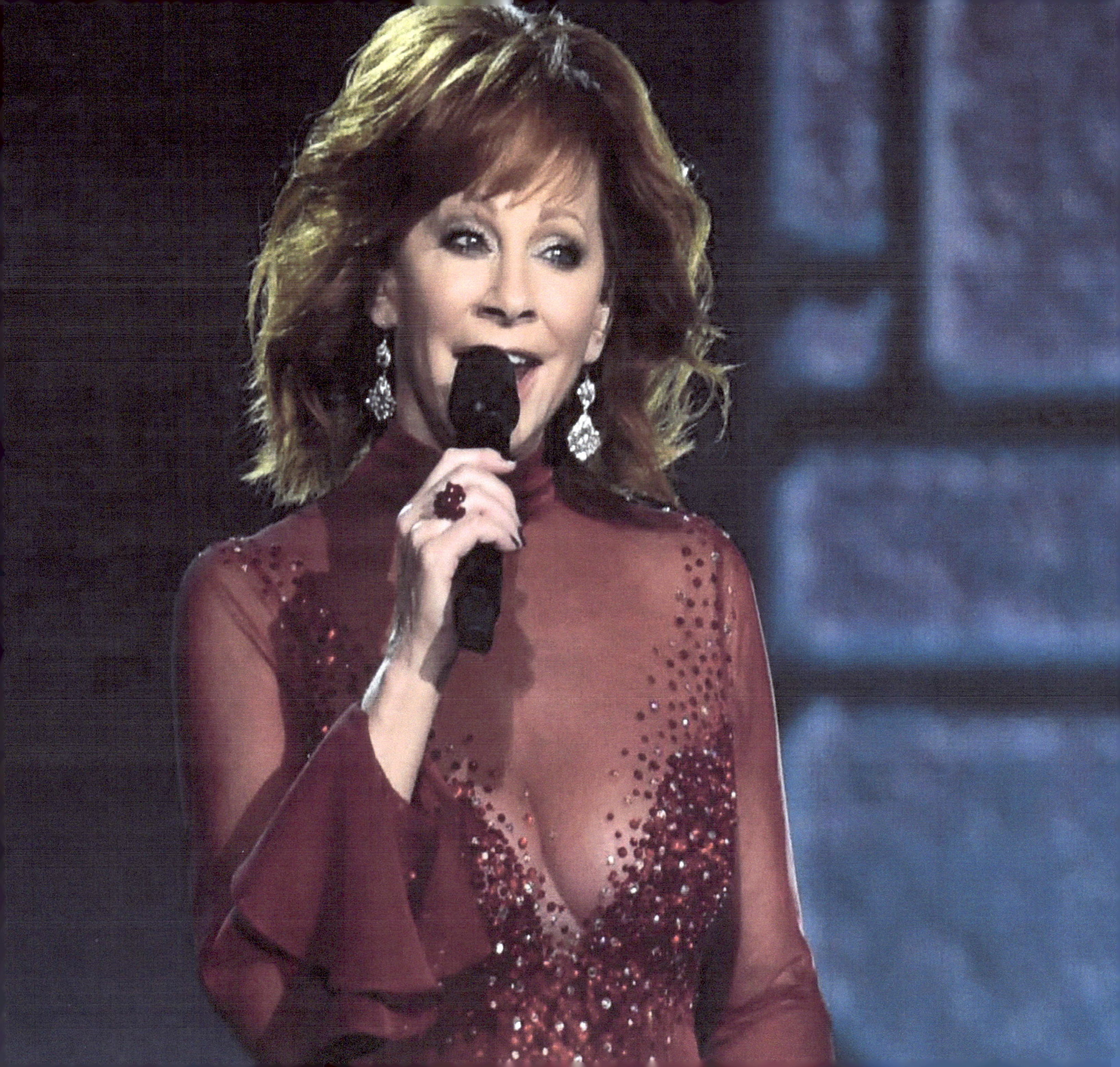

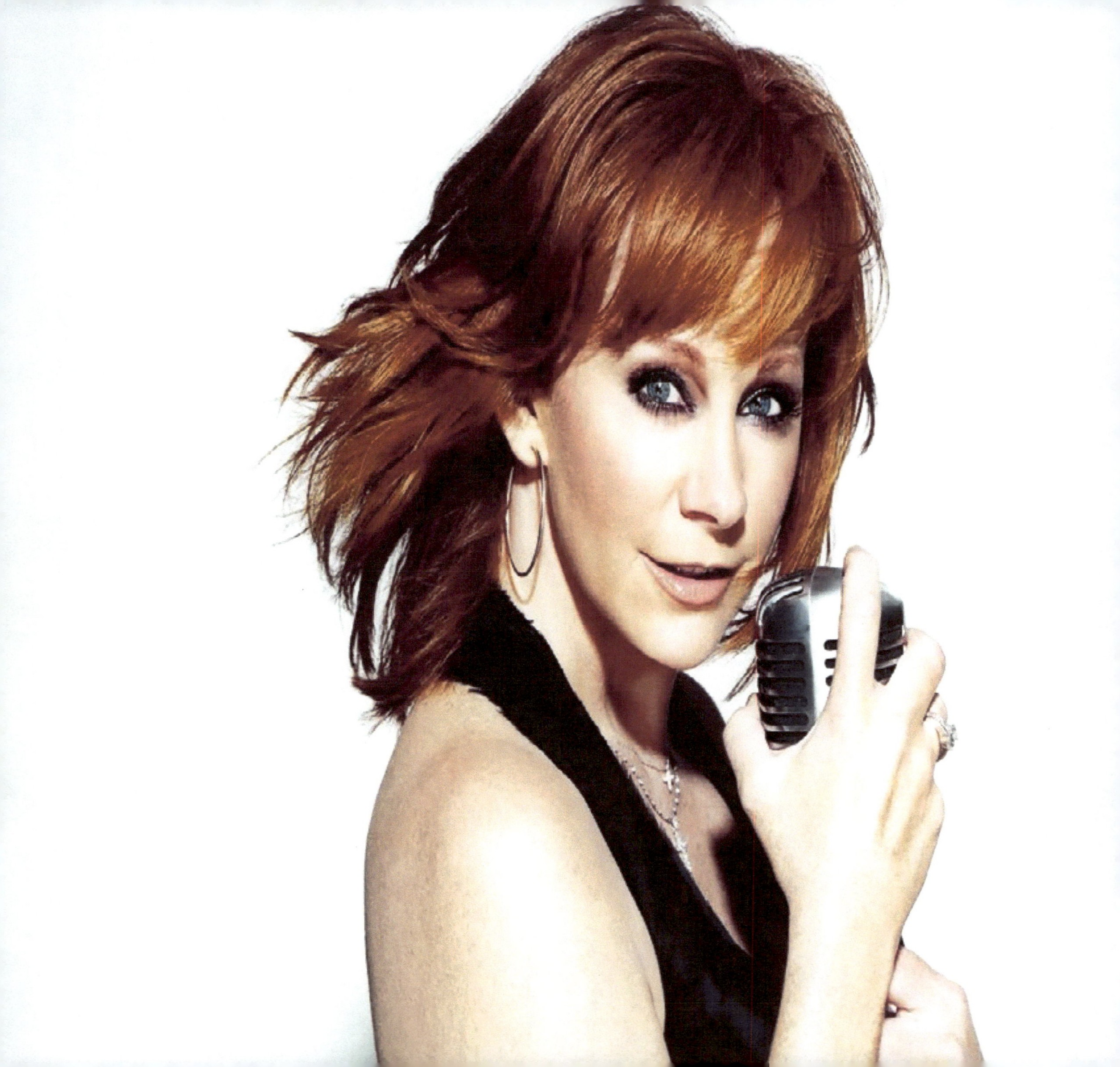

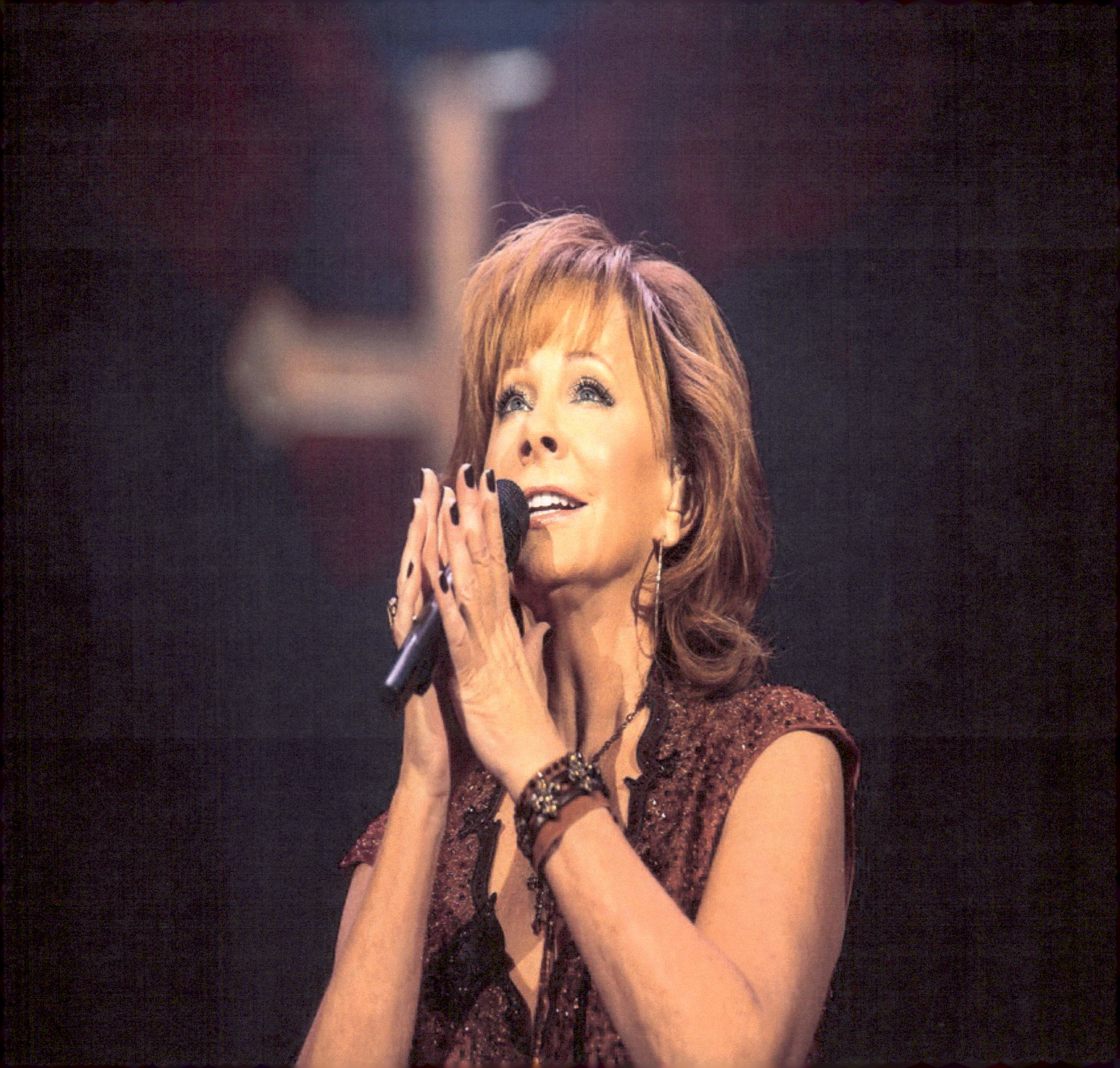

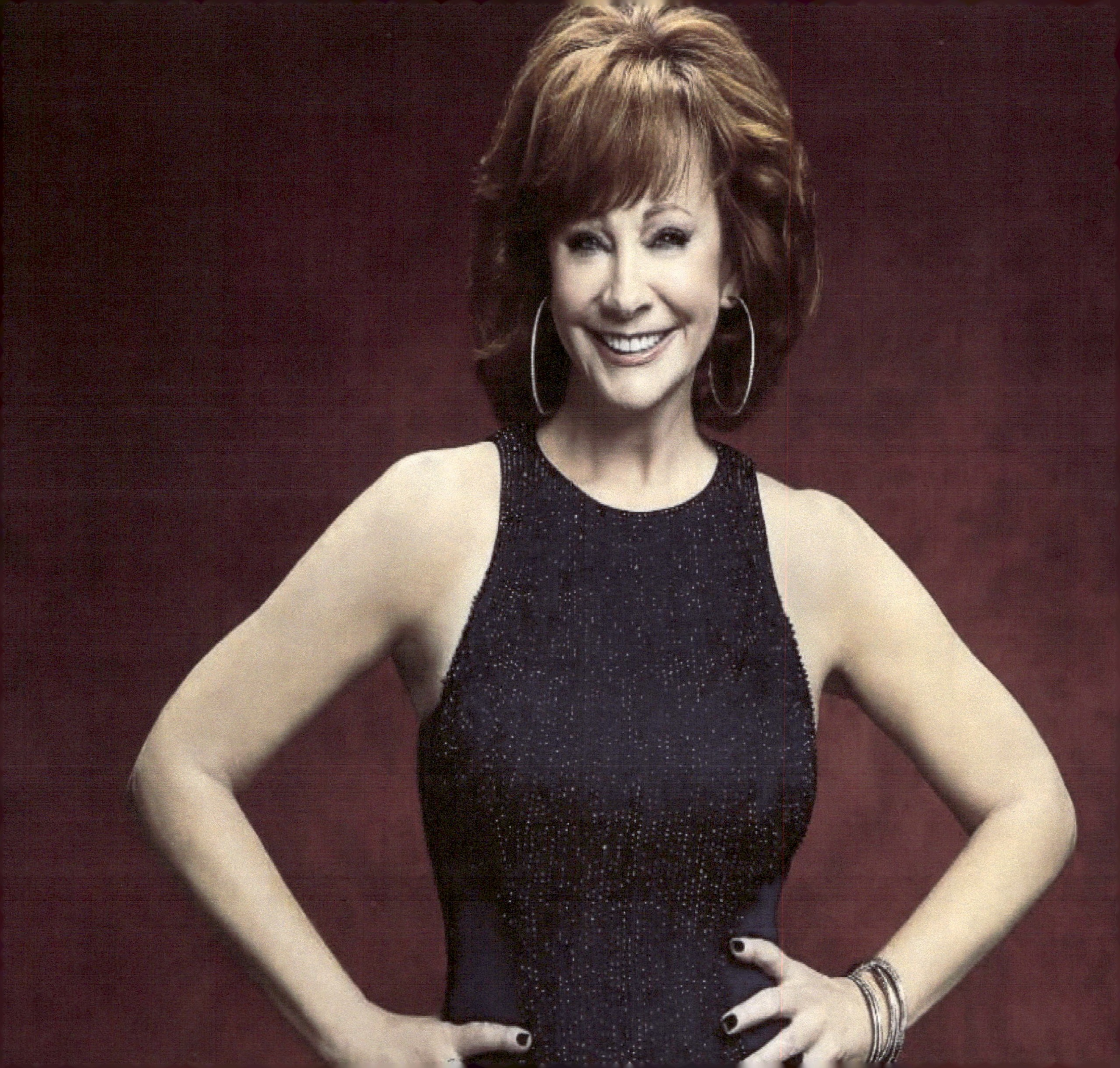

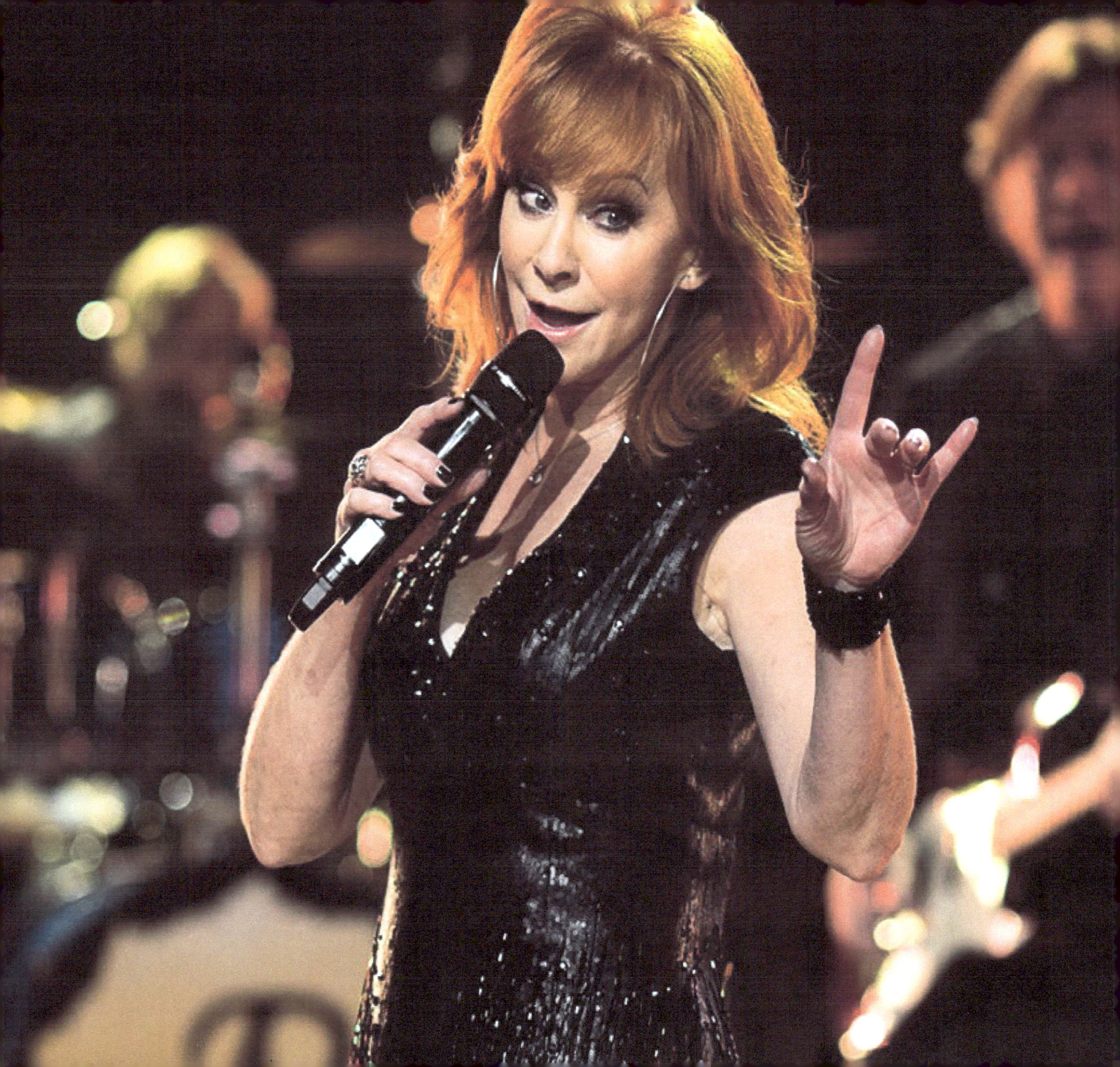

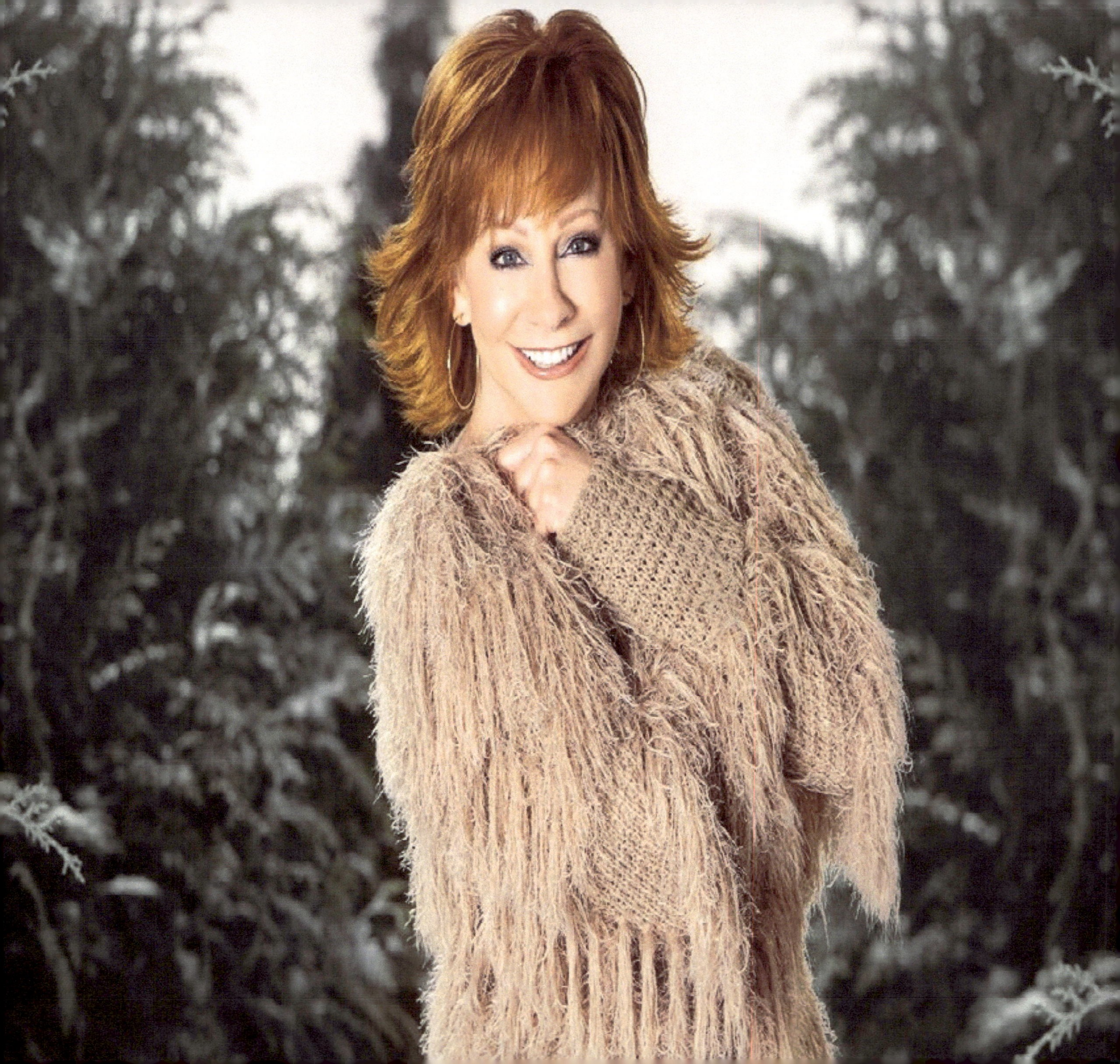

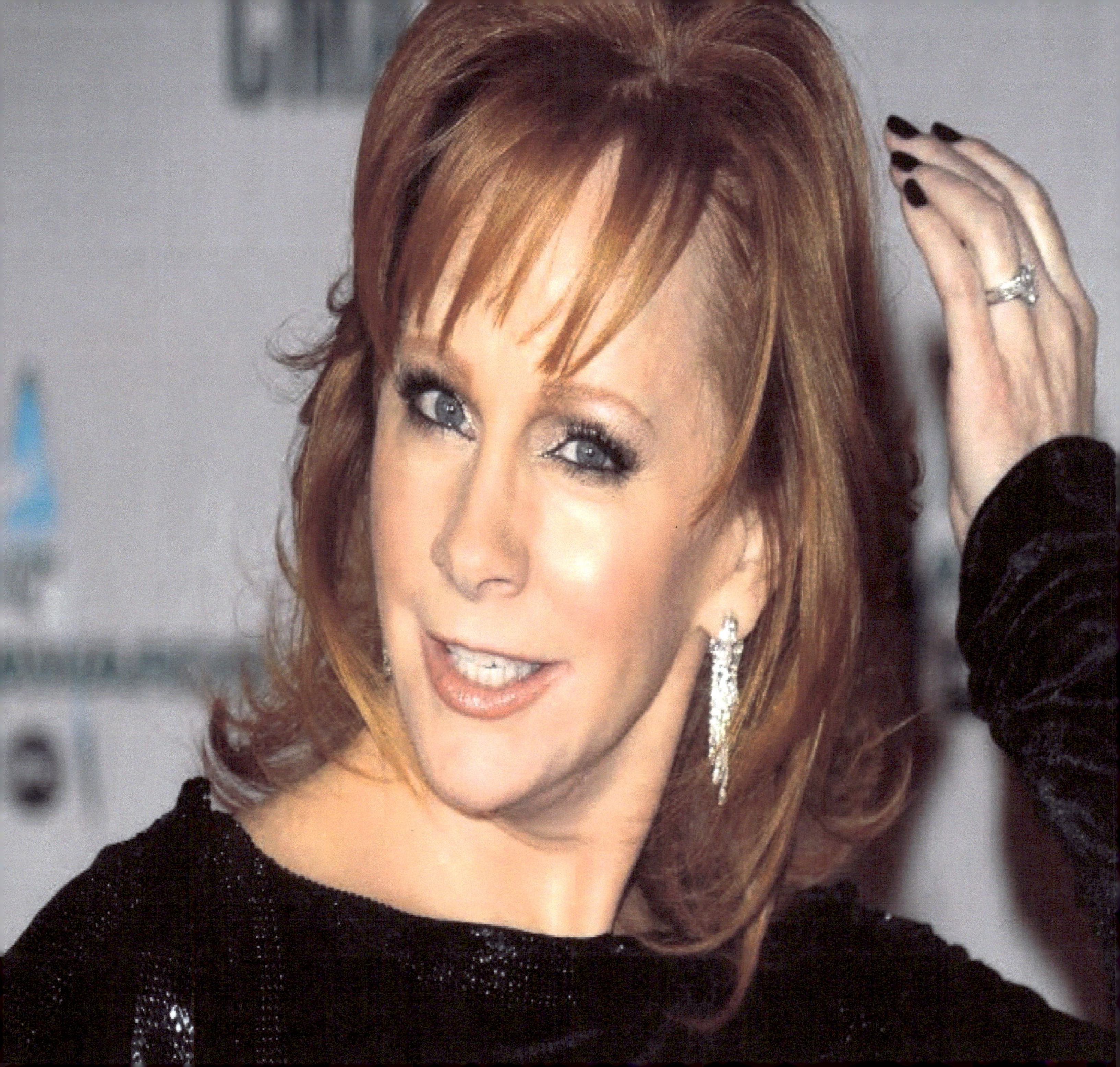

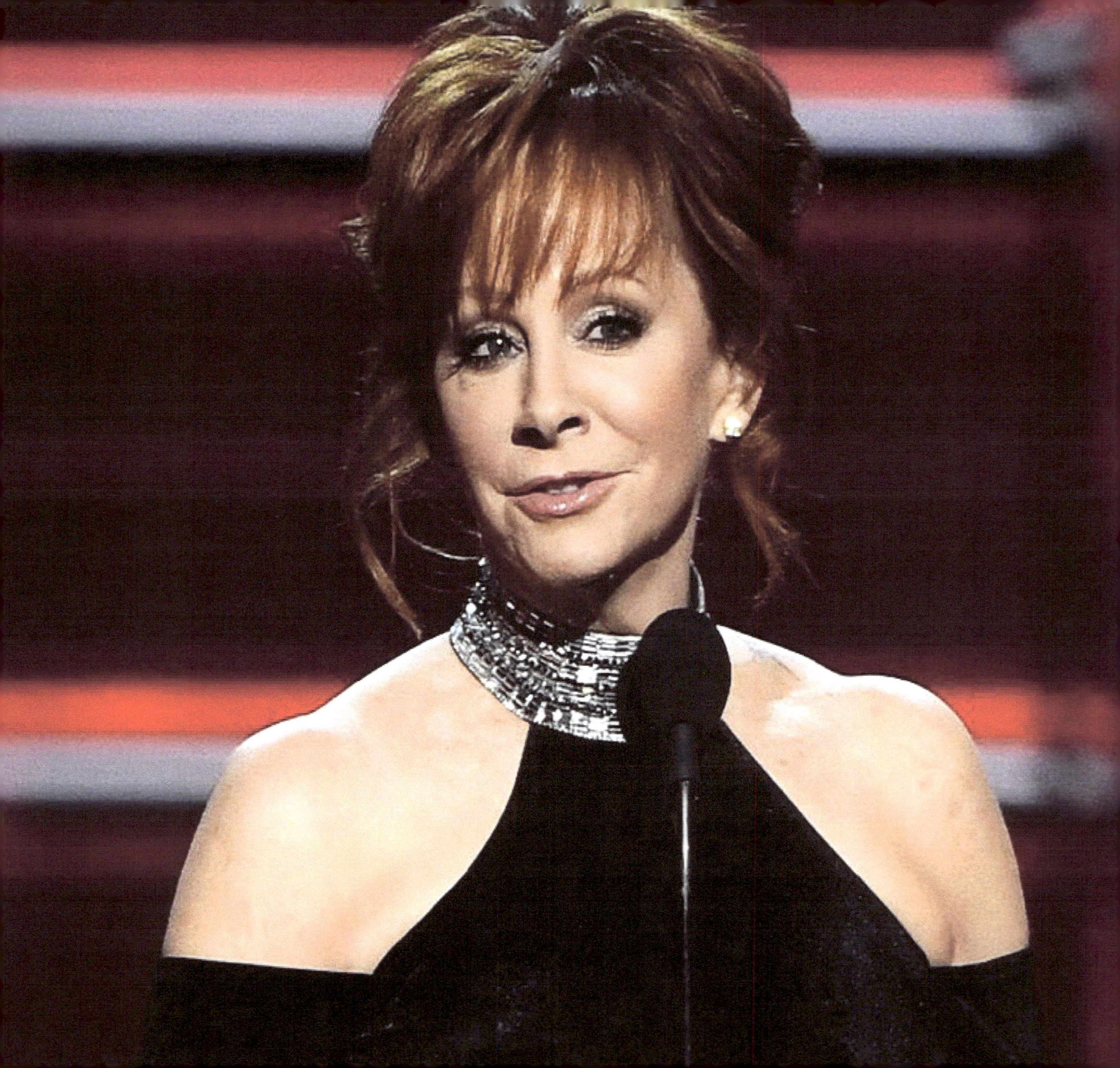

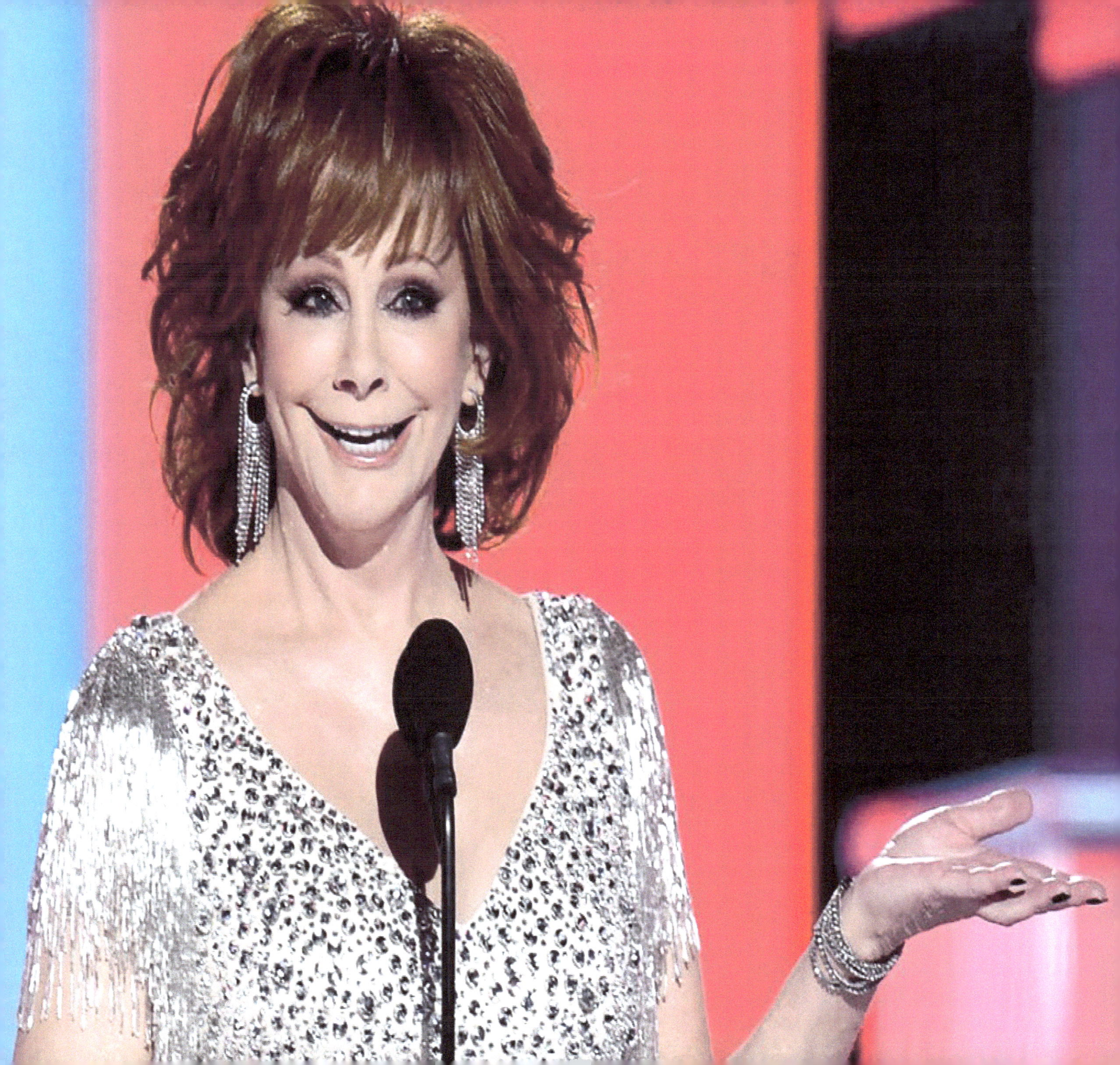

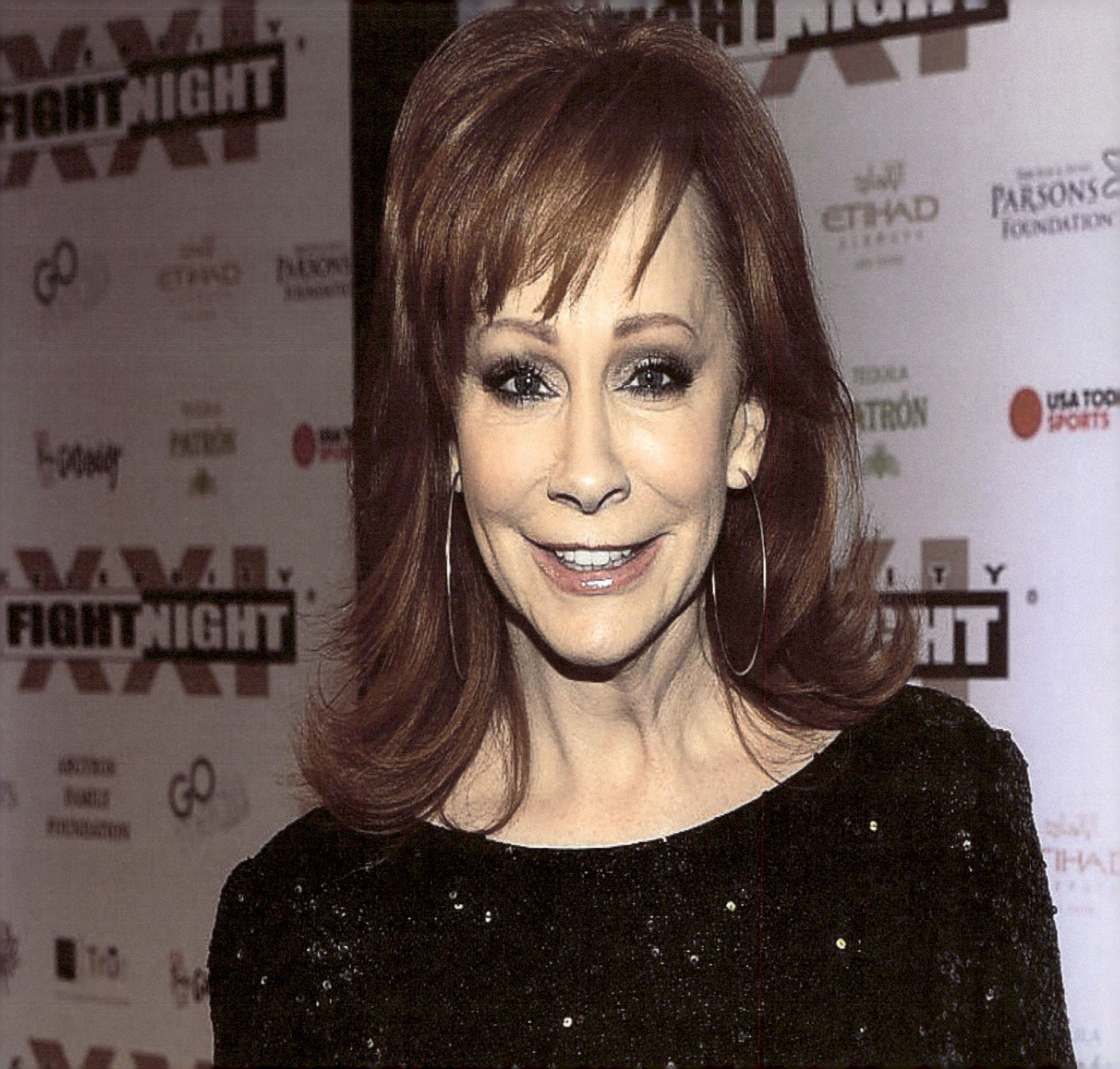
FIGHT NIGHT
XXI
ETIHAD
PARSONS
FOUNDATION
PATRÓN
USA TODAY SPORTS
FIGHT NIGHT
XXI

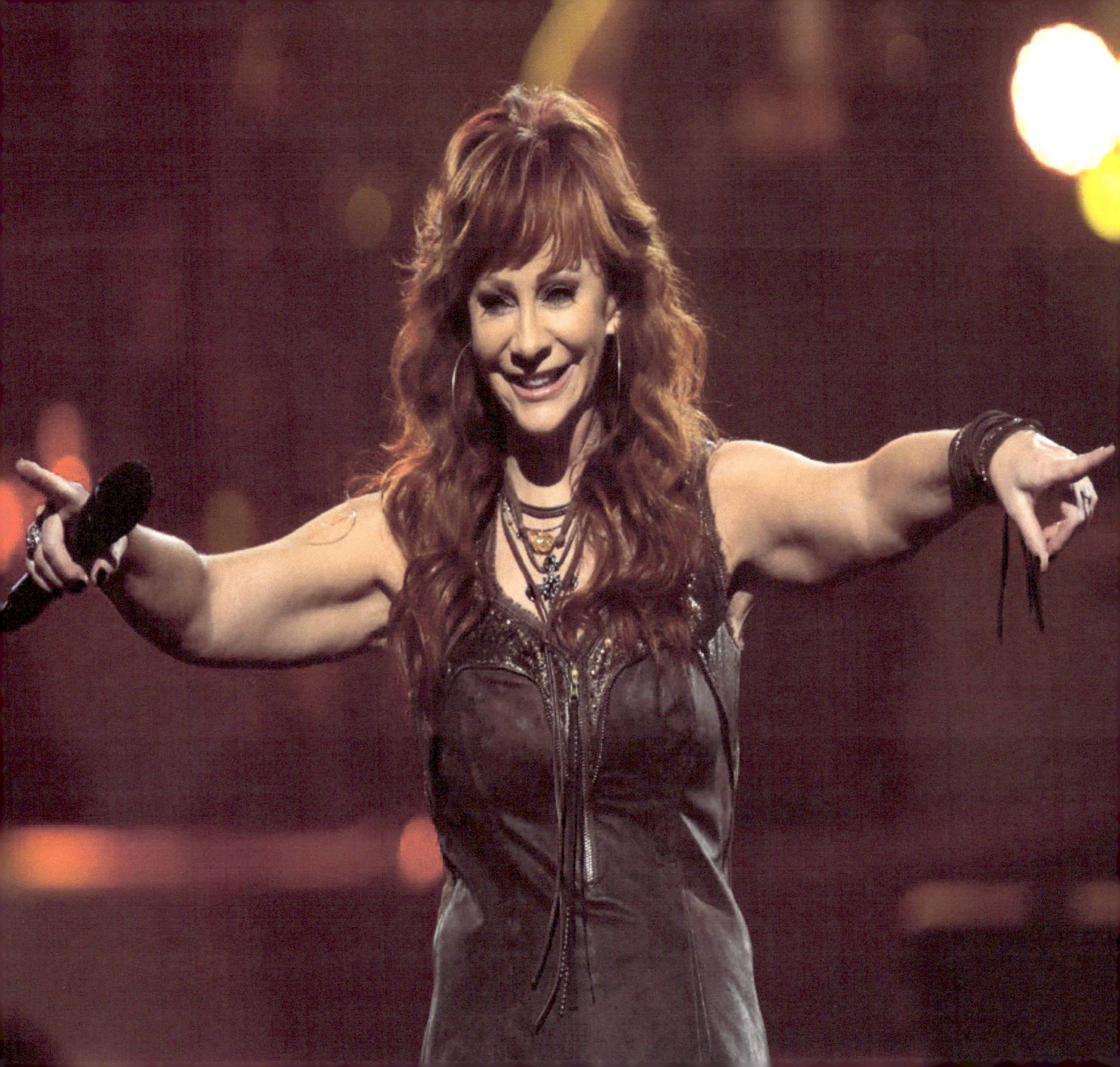

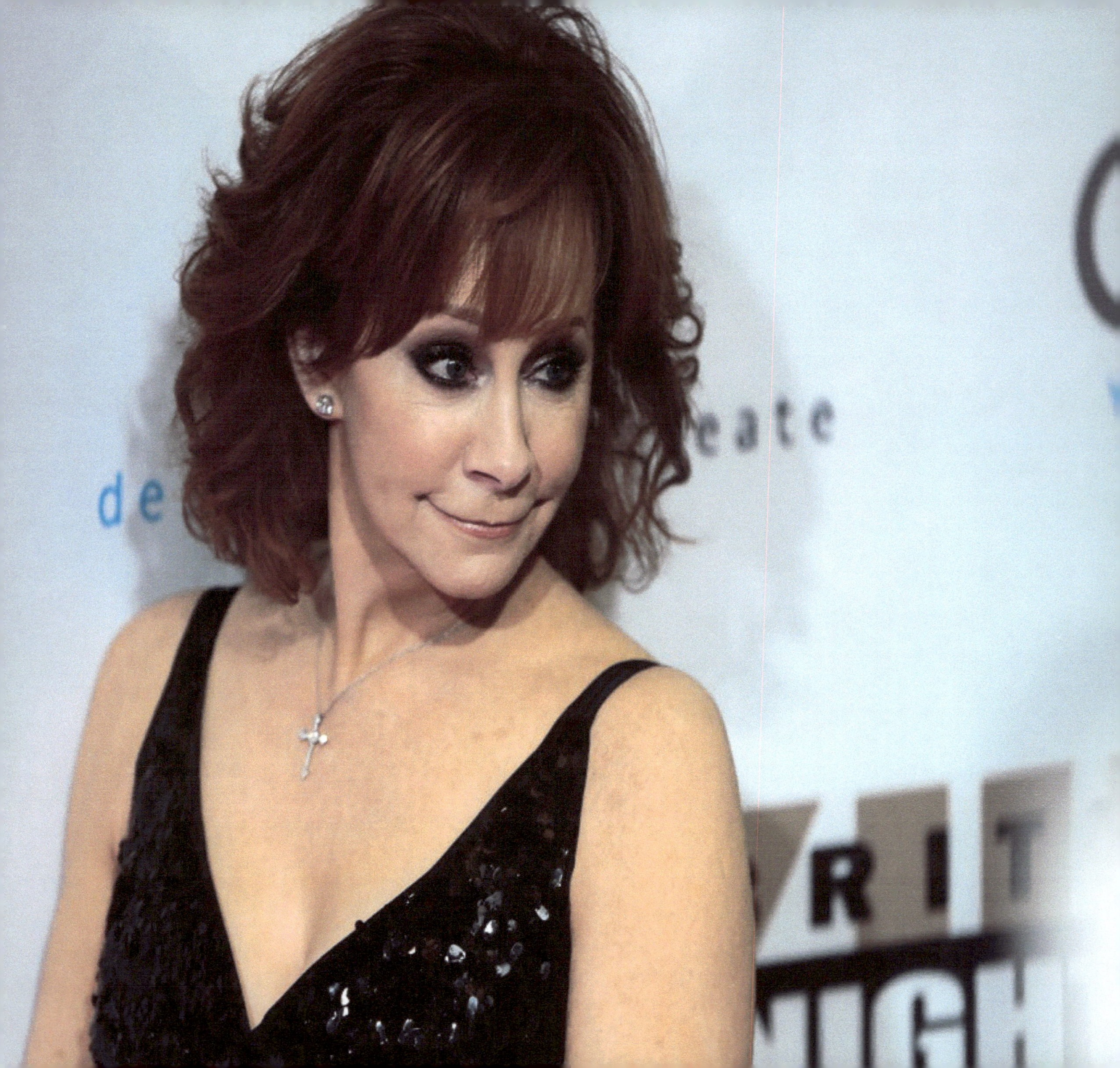
de
eate
RIT

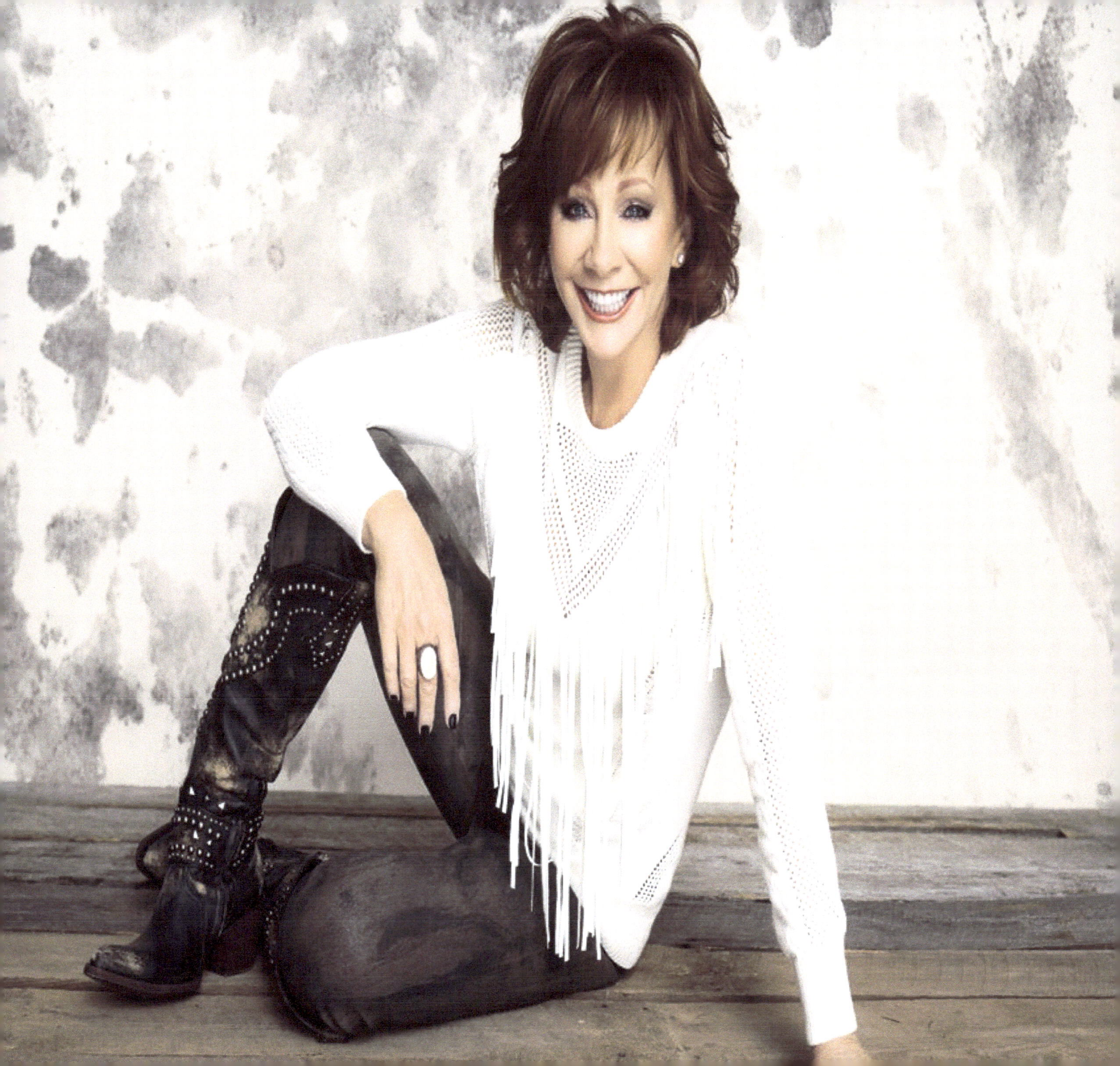

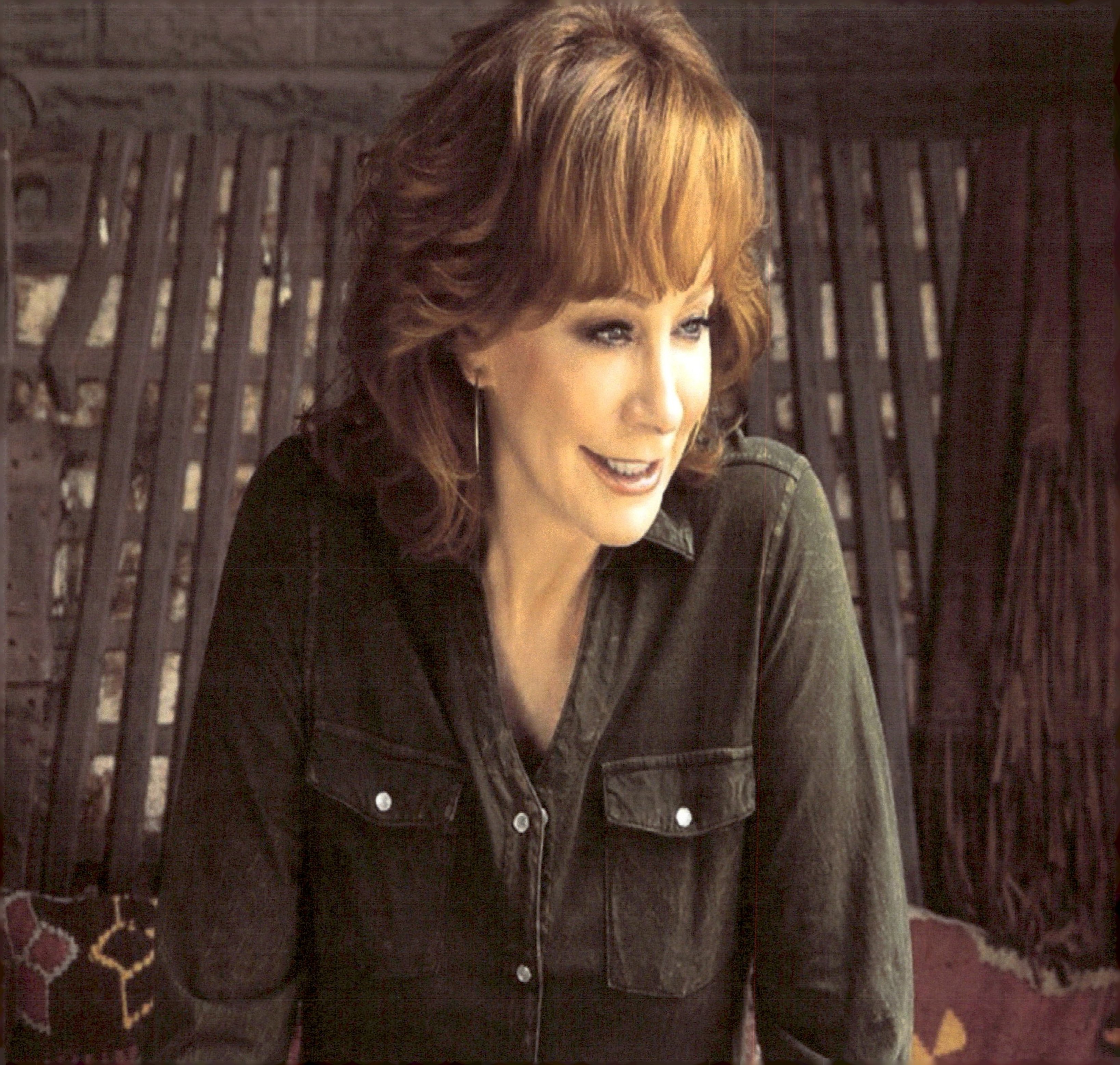

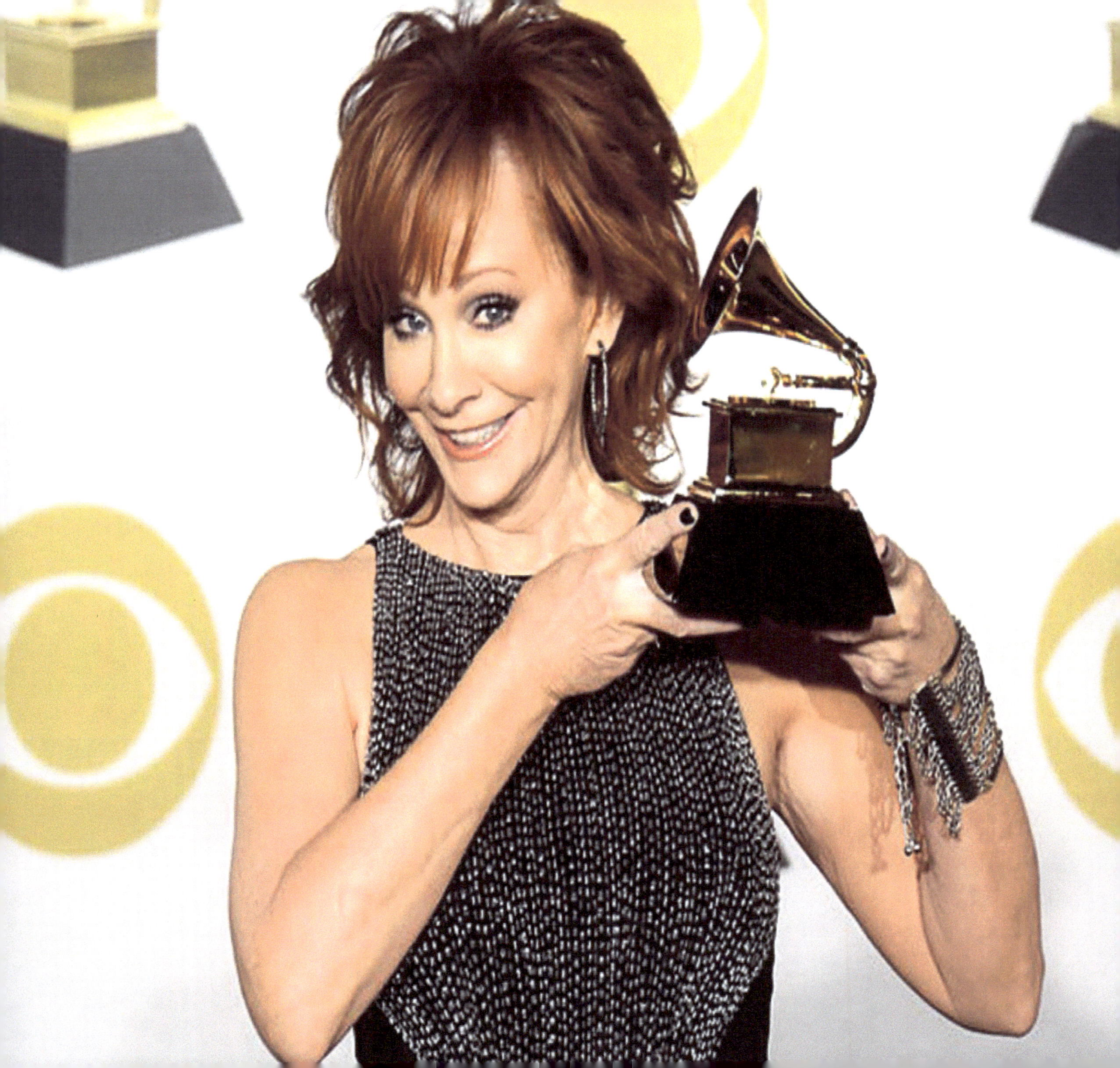

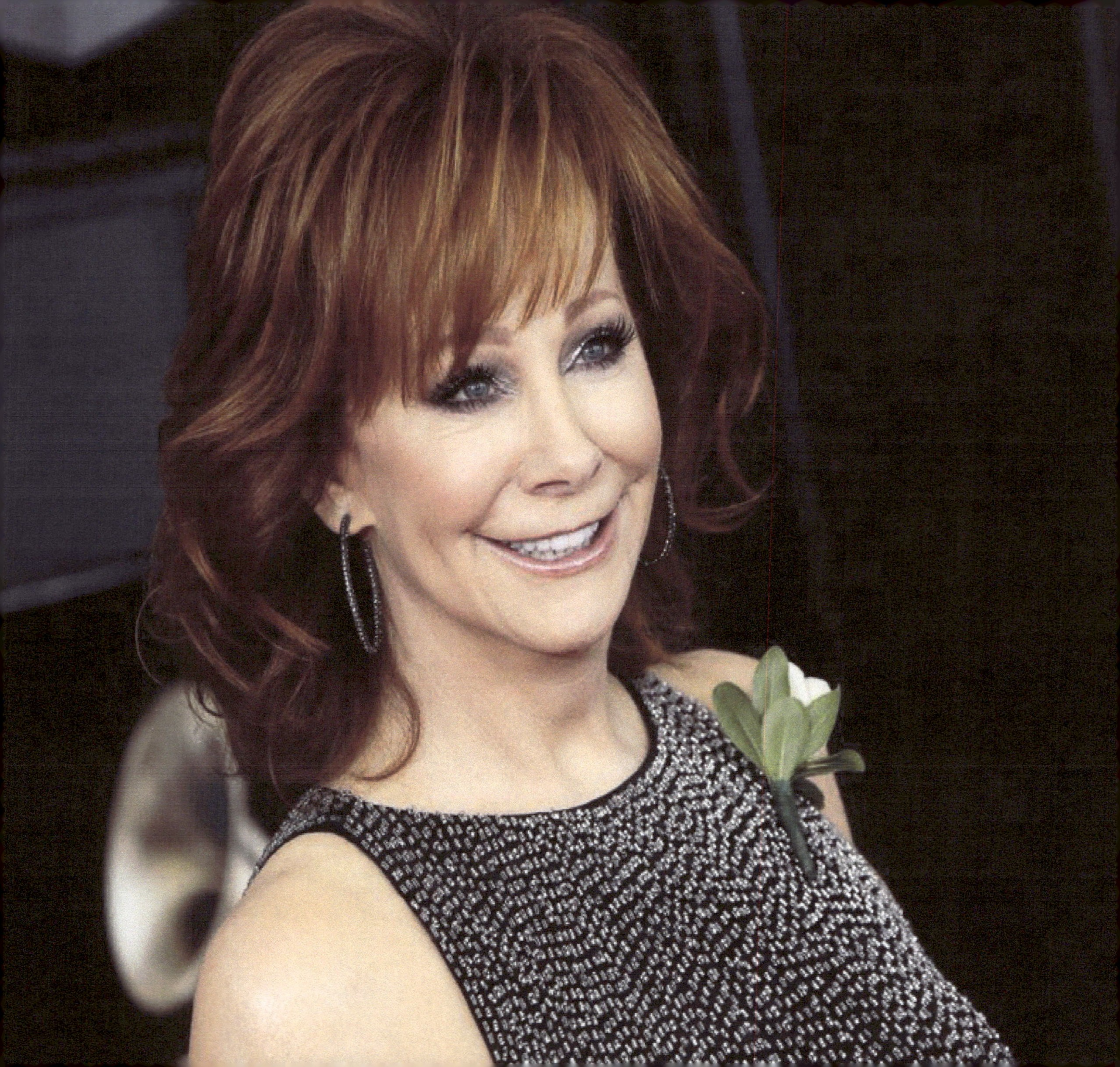

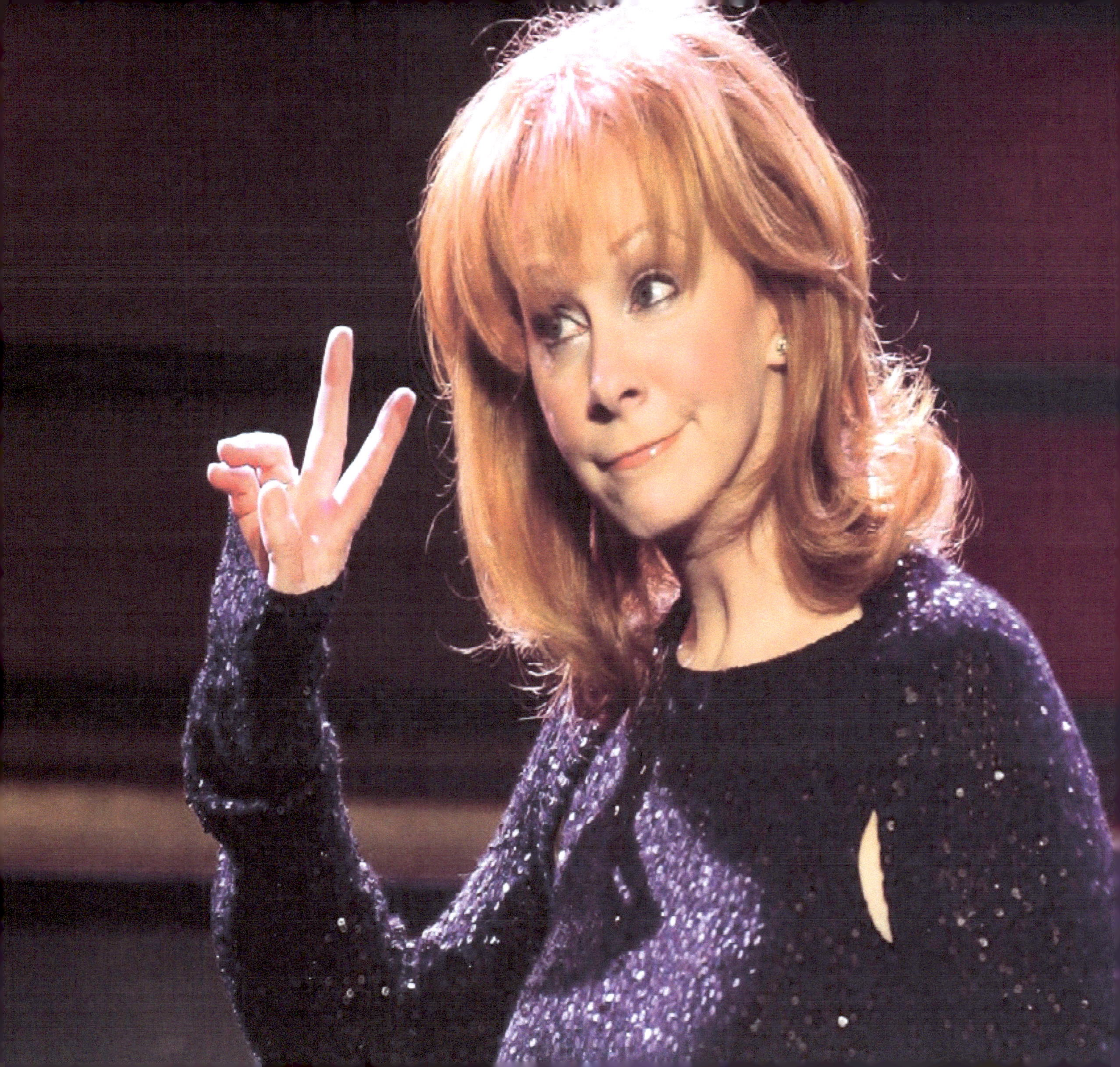

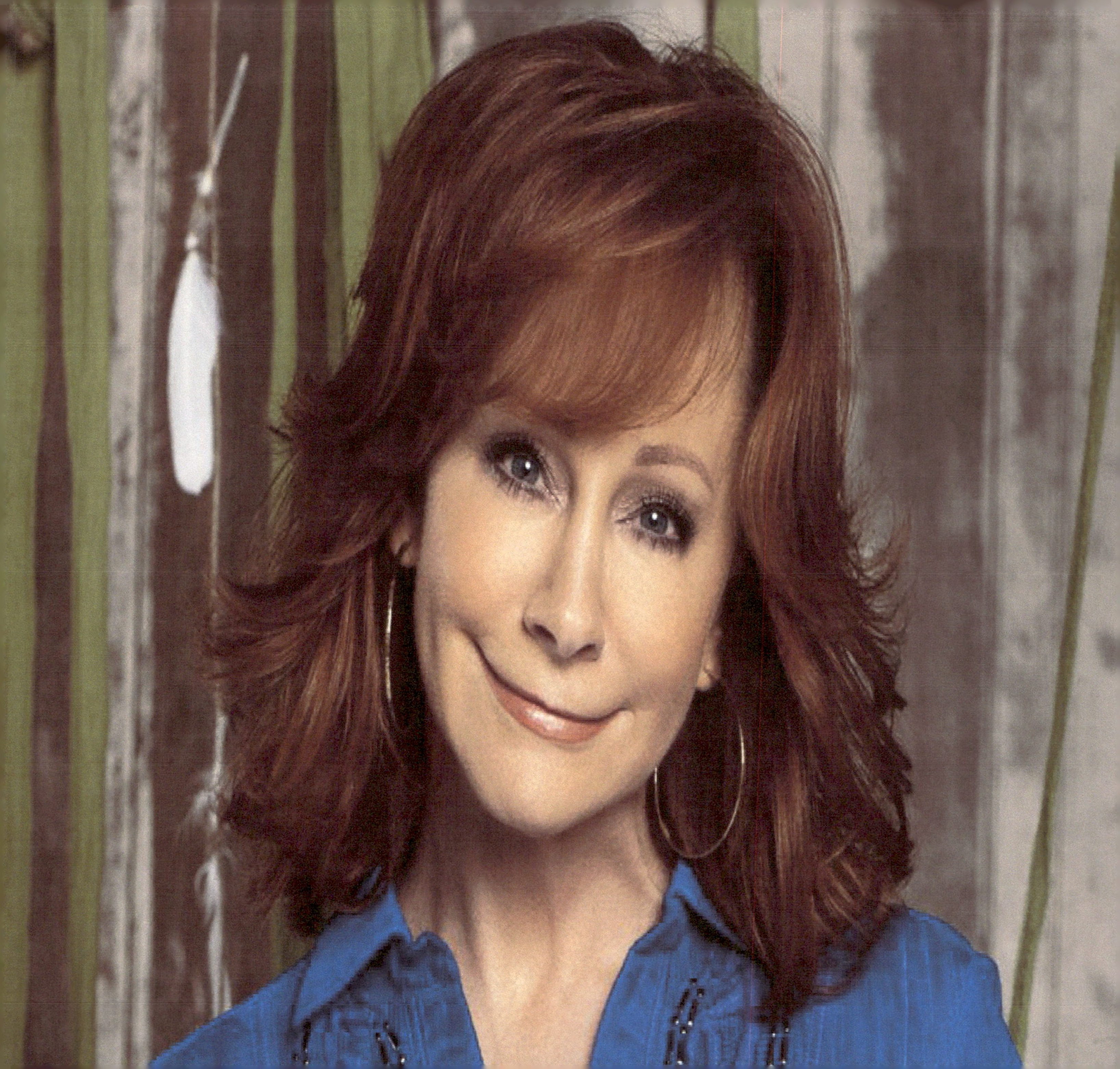

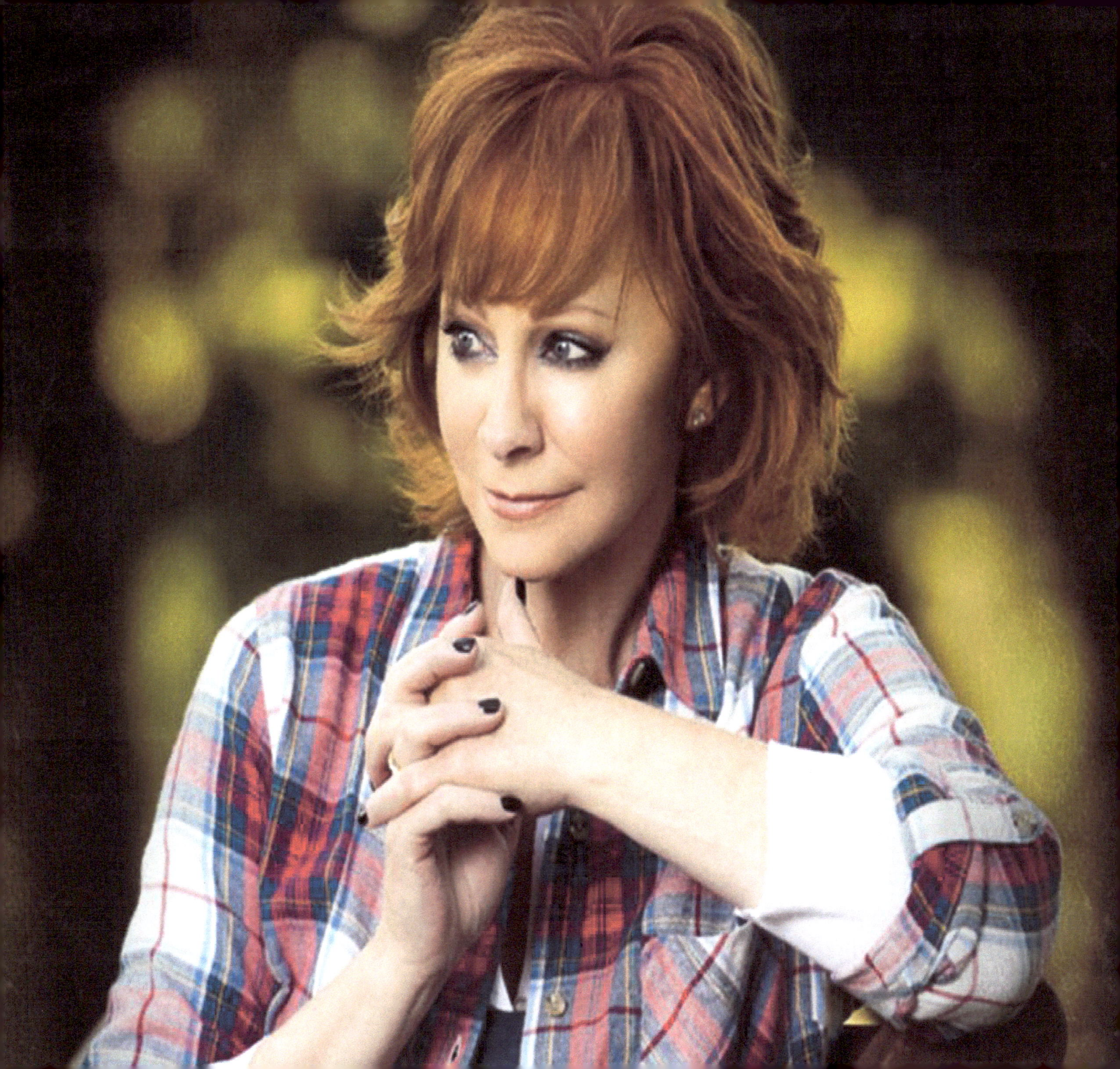

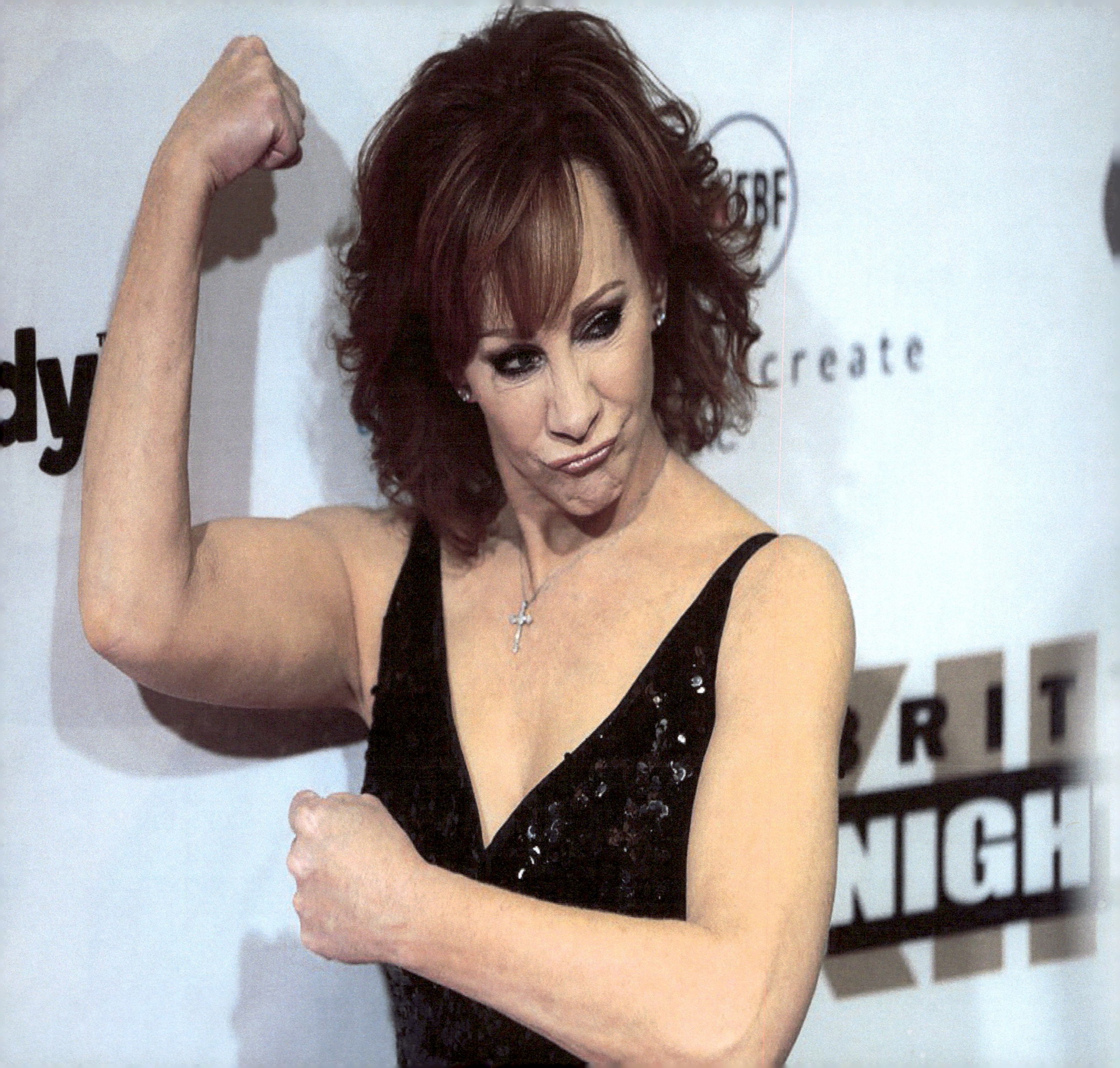
create

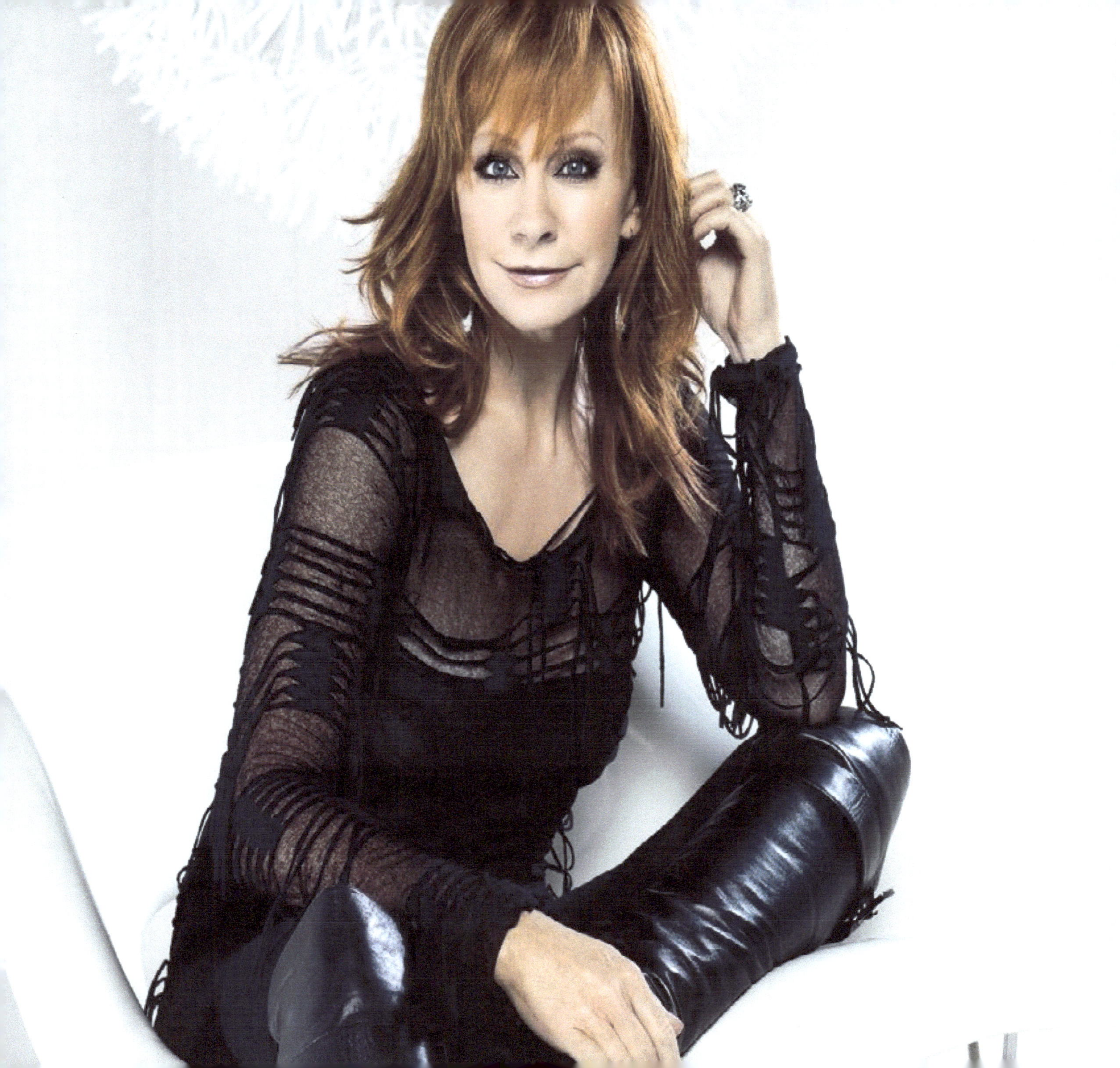

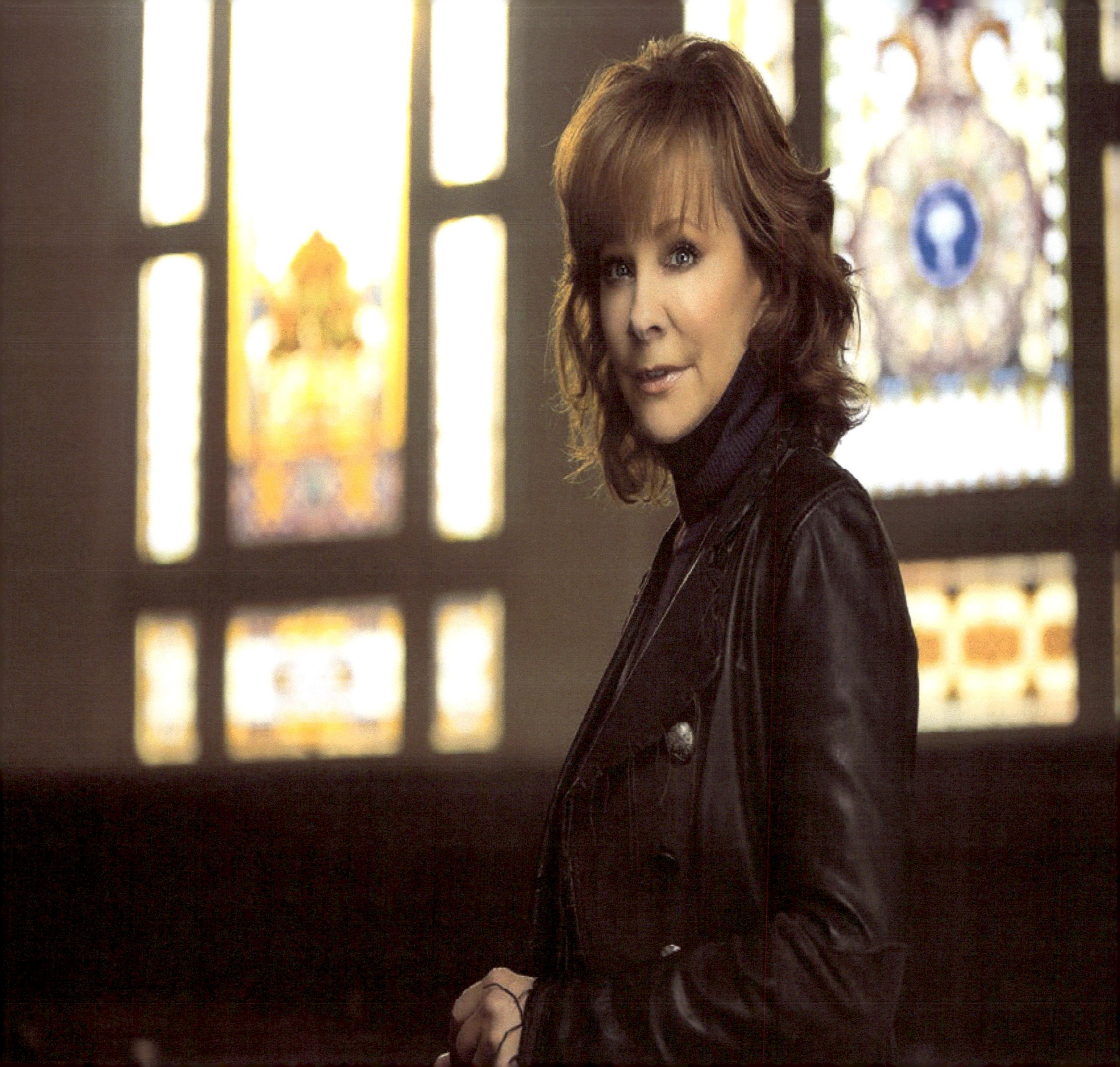

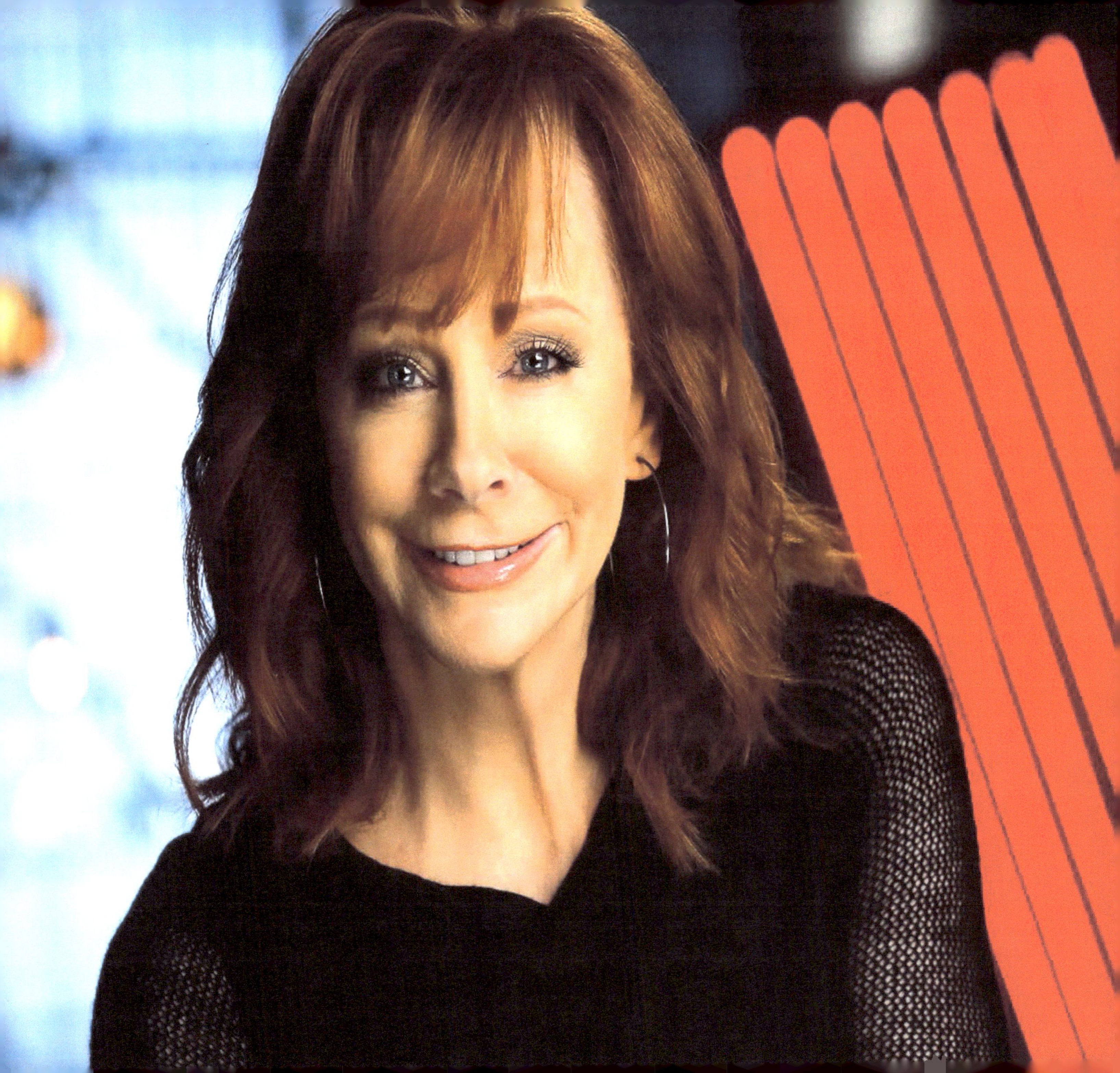

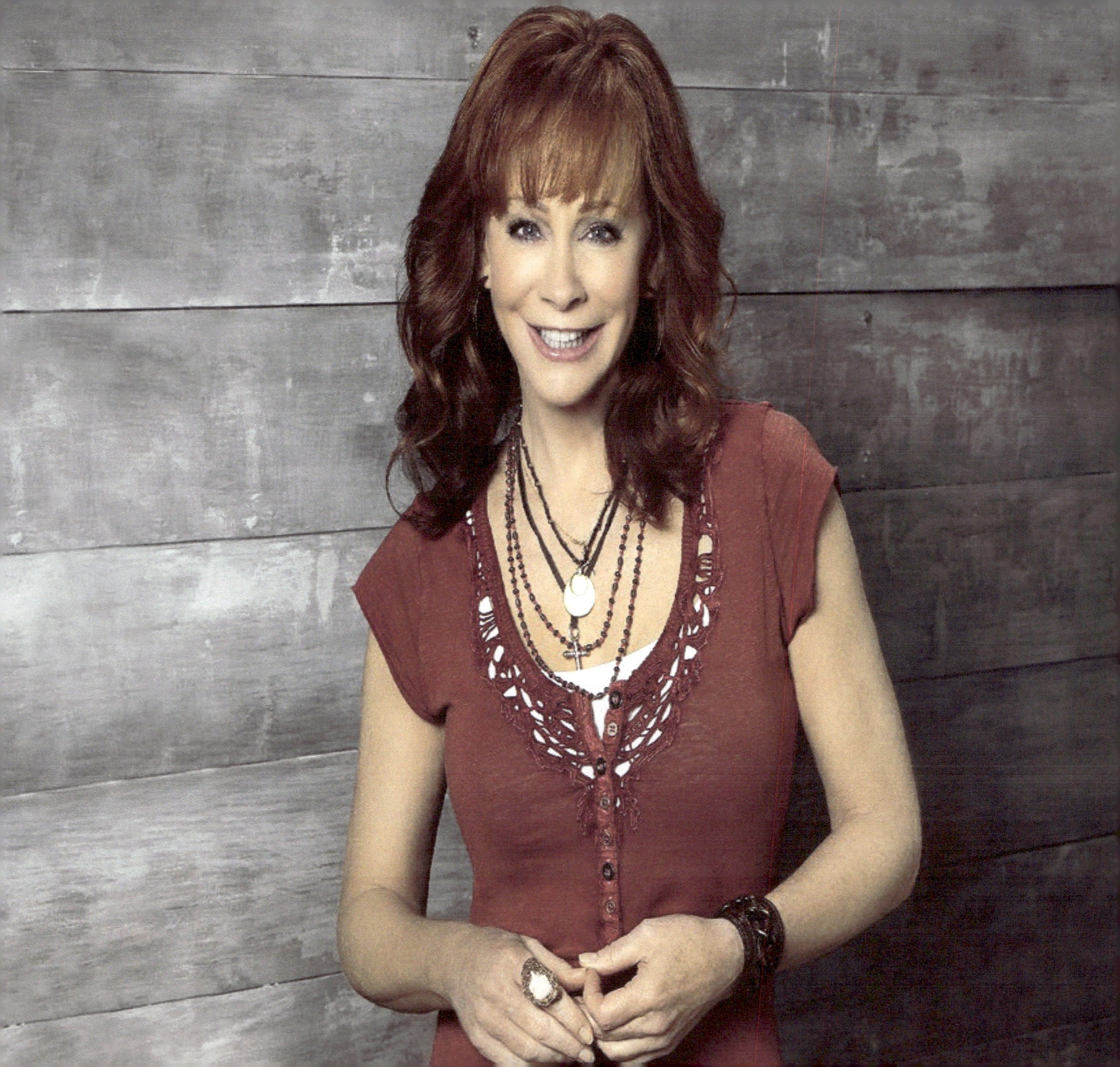

www.ingramcontent.com/pod-product-compliance
Lightning Source LLC
Chambersburg PA
CBHW051832210526
45473CB00005B/1840
9798367123890